Fun Crafts with Textures

Enslow Elementary

an imprint of

E **Enslow Publishers, Inc.**

40 Industrial Road   PO Box 38
Box 398   Aldershot
Berkeley Heights, NJ 07922 Hants GU12 6BP
USA   UK

http://www.enslow.com

Enslow Elementary, an imprint of Enslow Publishers, Inc.

Enslow Elementary® is a registered trademark of Enslow Publishers, Inc.

English edition copyright © 2006 by Enslow Publishers, Inc.

Translated from the Spanish edition by Toby S. McLellan, edited by Susana C. Schultz, of Strictly Spanish, LLC. Edited and produced by Enslow Publishers, Inc.

Library-in-Cataloging Publication Data

Ros, Jordina.
  [Texturas. English]
  Fun crafts with textures / Jordina Ros, Pere Estadella.
     p. cm. — (Arts and crafts fun)
  Originally published: Barcelona, Spain : Parramón, c2004.
  ISBN 0-7660-2654-X
  1. Art—Technique—Juvenile literature. 2. Texture (Art)—Juvenile literature. 3. Handicraft—Juvenile literature. I. Estadella, Pere. II. Title. III. Series.
  N7440.R67813 2005
  701'.8—dc22
                                    2005011223

Originally published in Spanish under the title *Las texturas*.
Copyright © 2004 PARRAMÓN EDICIONES, S.A., - World Rights.
Published by Parramón Ediciones, S.A., Barcelona, Spain.
Spanish edition produced by: Parramón Ediciones, S.A.
Authors: Jordina Ros and Pere Estadella
Collection and scale model design: Comando gráfico, S.L.
Photography: Estudio Nos & Soto
© the authorized reproductions, VEGAP, Barcelona
Parramón Ediciones, S.A., would like to give special thanks to Pol, Irene, Lluc, and Marina, who did such a wonderful job posing for the photographs in this book.

Printed in Spain

10 9 8 7 6 5 4 3 2 1

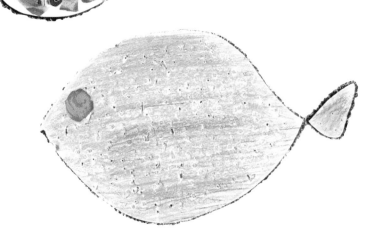

Fun Crafts with Textures

Table of Contents

6   What Is Texture?

7   Recognizing Textures

8   Creating Different Textures

9   Textures All Around Us

10   Discover Textures!

12   Open the Windows!

16   Three Chimneys

20   A Scratchy Plate

22   Like a Fish in Water

26   Smooth as Silk

28   The Ruby City

32   Now That's a Dirty Washcloth!

34   Crazy Train

36   Little House of Textures

40   An Unusual Doll

42   A Special Cake

45   "The Sock Collage" by Antoni Tàpies

46   Patterns

Make sure you have everything you need!
Before you start the craft, go over the list
of materials.

Be careful with sharp objects!
You may be using sharp tools, such as scissors
or something to punch holes with. Always ask
an adult for permission or for help.

Wait for the paint to dry!
When an exercise requires paint, you must wait
until it is completely dry before you can continue.
You can ask an adult to help you dry the work
carefully with a blow dryer.

Imagination
If you come up with a new idea while working
on these crafts, tell a teacher or another adult.
Together you can create new crafts that are all
your own.

What Is Texture?

Texture describes what something feels like when you touch it. Different things have different textures depending on what they are made of. A metal object will probably have a smooth texture. A wool sweater has a fuzzy texture.

Touch is the main sense you use to recognize texture. Sometimes you can also tell the texture of something by looking at it. Textures can be rough, smooth, scratchy, hard, or soft. What other textures can you think of?

The bark of a tree has a rough texture.

When you pet a puppy, does his fur feel soft and silky, or curly and coarse?

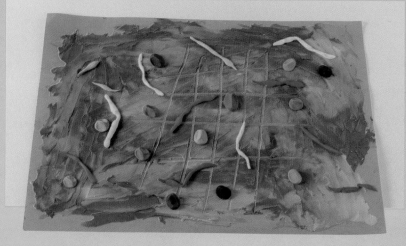

It is fun to work with different textures. Look at this clay!

Recognizing Textures

If you are a good detective, you can discover the texture of any material—with your eyes closed!

Textures are mostly identified by the sense of touch.

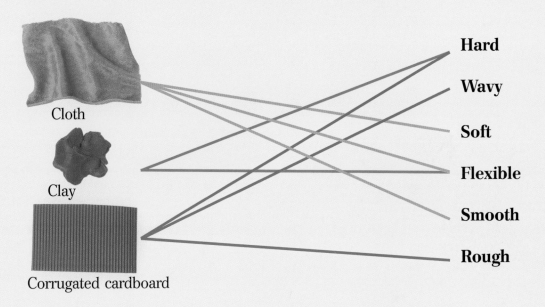

Cloth

Clay

Corrugated cardboard

Hard

Wavy

Soft

Flexible

Smooth

Rough

Sometimes you can identify textures by sight. The way light shines on a surface can help you see what kind of texture it has. A bright, shiny surface is probably very smooth. A dull surface may have a soft or rough texture.

Other things, such as wind, can also help you figure out what kind of texture something has—or even change its texture! How?

Sometimes the ocean's surface is very choppy, and sometimes it looks smooth. That's partly because of wind!

Creating Different Textures

You can create different textures using different materials and tools—including your own hands!

You can use your hands to crumple, tear, or scratch.

You can use tools to make textures.

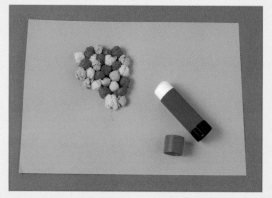

You can use different materials to create textures.

You can use colored pencils or paints to create different textures.

You can even change an object's texture by changing its size. Doesn't a balloon feel different after you blow it up?

Look at the hair on your hand with a magnifying glass. How many lines are there? What is the texture like? How would you create that texture on paper?

Stick tiny pieces of clay onto the smooth surface of an egg. Now it's bumpy!

Textures All Around Us

You can see all kinds of things on a trip through a city, to the country, to the beach, or to the mountains. If you stop to touch them, you will find that they all have different textures.

Just by looking and touching you can tell how many different textures are all around us.

The ocean has calm waters or choppy waves.

The desert has fine sand and wavy dunes.

Glaciers have smooth, cold ice.

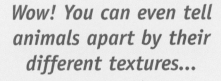
The woods have rough, hard trees and smooth leaves.

Wow! You can even tell animals apart by their different textures...

Cats have smooth fur— even big cats!

An elephant's skin is hard and rough.

What do you think fish scales are like?

Discover Textures!

What you will need...

Blue poster board
White construction paper
Corrugated cardboard
Leaf
Rock
Shell
Glue stick
Colored pencils
Marker

Do you want to make textures show up on a sheet of paper?

Divide the white paper into four parts. Place the leaf below one part. Rub a green pencil over it to transfer the leaf's texture to the paper.

Put the corrugated cardboard under another part of the paper. Rub over it with a red pencil.

Put the shell below a third part of the paper. Carefully rub a dark red pencil over it.

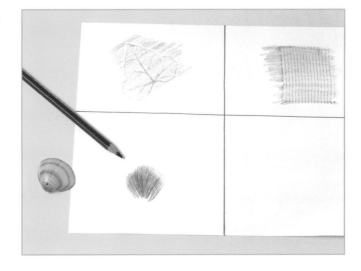

And what texture will appear in the last part?

Place the rock under the last part and rub over it with the black pencil.

Glue the white sheet onto the blue poster board. Then place each object near its colored texture. How does each texture look compared to how it feels?

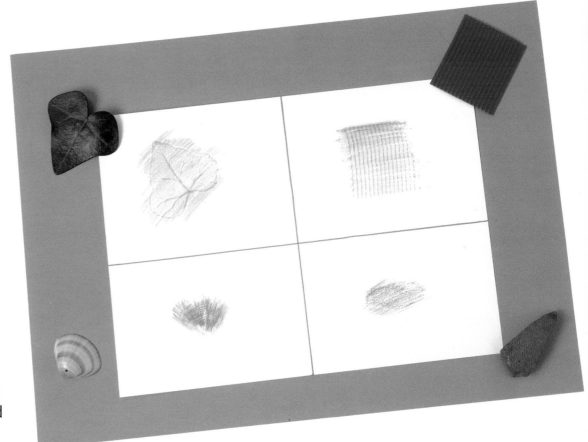

YOU CAN TRY

Try making a greeting card! Use crayons or colored pencils to rub the texture of an object you like onto one half of a piece of paper. Fold the paper, then write your greeting inside.

Open the Windows!

What you will need...

Orange poster board
Blue corrugated cardboard
Aluminum foil
Clear plastic wrap
Red cellophane
Green coated paper
Scissors
Glue stick
Pencil
Hole puncher or scissors
Tracing paper
Pattern (page 46)

Do you want to make a game for your friends to learn how to tell different textures apart?

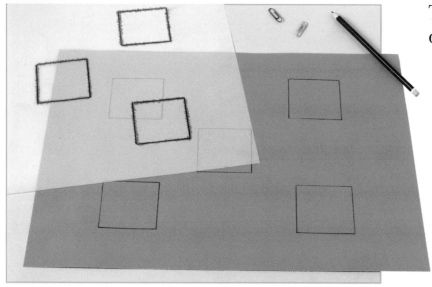

Trace five windows of the pattern (page 46) onto the orange poster board.

Let's open the windows!

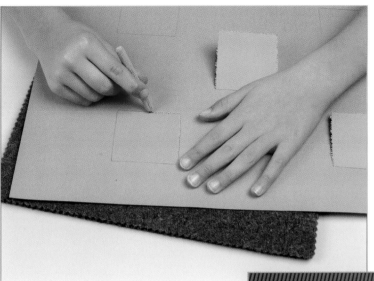

Use a hole puncher or scissors to carefully cut each of the windows on three sides. Leave the tops of the windows uncut.

Now for the different textures!

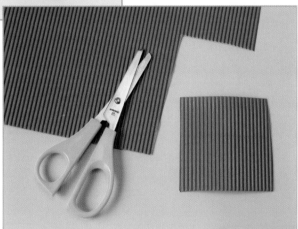

Cut a piece of blue corrugated cardboard a little bigger than one of the windows.

Also cut a piece of aluminum foil and a piece of coated green paper about the same size as the cardboard.

All of these materials have different textures, right?

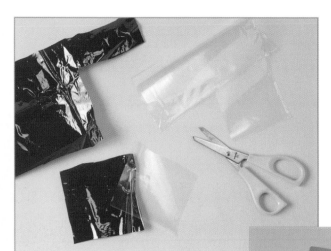

Now cut a piece of red cellophane and a piece of clear plastic wrap about the same size as the cardboard.

Glue the different pieces of material onto the orange poster board, one behind each window.

Turn the poster board over. Finish decorating it with the rest of the materials you have.

Touch the material hiding under each window. What is its texture?

TIP
If you can't find colored corrugated cardboard, you can color or paint regular corrugated cardboard any color you like!

Three Chimneys

What you will need...

Black poster board
Three toilet-paper tubes
Colored feathers
Sawdust
Pink poster paint
White glue
Paintbrush
Three plastic containers

Would you like to make three chimneys with different textures?

Put sawdust in one container, colored feathers in another, and a mixture of white glue and pink paint in the third.

Use the paintbrush to spread a coat of white glue on one of the cardboard tubes. Dip the tube into the container with sawdust.

Spread glue on another tube. Glue the colored feathers onto it.

Dip the last cardboard tube into the container with white glue mixed with pink paint.

Such different textures! Let's put them on a base that's just right for each one...

Paint a small circle of the glue mixed with pink paint onto the black poster board. Attach the matching tube to it.

Next to this, make another circle of white glue. Glue on some feathers, then add the matching tube.

Make a third circle of white glue. Put sawdust on it, then glue the last tube on.

The tube with colored glue has a smooth texture and looks like plastic. The one with feathers has a very soft texture, and the one with sawdust is very rough. Now you have three chimneys with three textures!

YOU CAN TRY

Try making more textures! What if you made a chimney with sand on it? Or balloons? Or grass?

A Scratchy Plate

What you will need...
Fine-grained sandpaper
Coarse-grained sandpaper
Yellow and orange crayons
Plastic or paper plate
Glue stick

*You probably know that sandpaper is used to make wood smooth.
For this craft, however, we will work with the sandpaper's rough texture.*

Color some of the coarse-grained sandpaper orange. Now color some of the fine-grained sandpaper yellow.

Can you see how different the textures look?

Tear both pieces of sandpaper into small pieces.

Use the crayons to color your plastic or paper plate. What kind of texture does it have?

Glue the torn pieces of colored sandpaper to the plate. Also glue on some sandpaper that you didn't color.

The rough texture shows better on the colored sandpaper. Can you see the difference?

YOU CAN TRY
Try coloring all kinds of different things to help you see their textures better. Try making a craft like this using different kinds of colored leaves instead of colored sandpaper!

Like a Fish in Water

What you will need...

Two white poster boards
Two soft printed cloths
Blue poster paint
Crayons
Sponge
Glue stick
Hole puncher or scissors
Scissors
Pencil
Tracing paper
Pattern (page 47)

Do you know that fish scales have a texture that can feel very smooth or very rough, depending on how you touch them?

Paint one of the white poster boards with a sponge and blue paint, to look like the bottom of the sea.

Trace the two outlines of fish from the pattern (page 47) onto the other sheet of white poster board. Punch or cut the fish shapes out from the poster board.

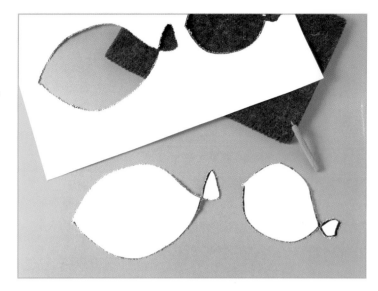

Now punch holes all over the surface of the large fish.

Turn it over so that the bumpy side is showing. Color it with crayons.

Now you have a rough fish! Do you want a smoother one?

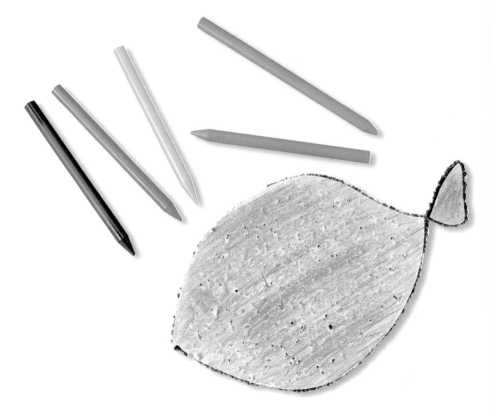

Cut the smooth cloths into pieces.

Glue the pieces of cloth all over
the surface of the small fish.

**Now you have a fish with smooth scales
and a fish with rough scales!**

Glue an extra piece of cloth onto the large
fish for an eye, then glue the two fish onto
the blue painted poster board. Now they
are happily swimming in the sea!

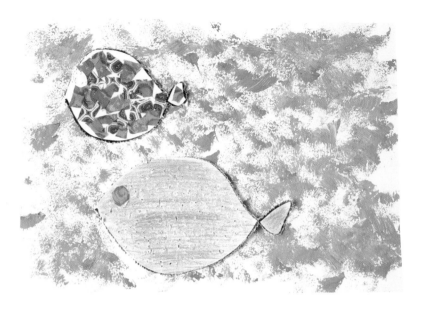

If you have a chance to look at a real aquarium, you will see that real fish also have different textures.

YOU CAN TRY

Try making different animals with different textures. How about a smooth frog and a bumpy toad? Or a puppy with curly, coarse fur and a kitten with smooth fur?

Smooth as Silk

What you will need...

White poster board
Tissue paper (various colors)
Glue stick

Tear some of the tissue paper
into small pieces.

*Touch the tissue paper before you
begin. What a smooth texture!*

Spread a thick coat of glue onto the
front of the white poster board.

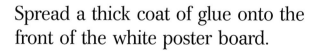

Stick the torn pieces of tissue paper onto the poster board. Cover the whole surface.

How pretty—and how smooth! Do you want to change this texture?

Tear some of the remaining tissue paper into strips. Crumple and roll them up like sticks, then glue them onto the poster board.

Run your fingers over your artwork again. It is not so smooth anymore! Now it is bumpy and rough.

YOU CAN TRY
What else can you do to add more textures to your artwork? Be creative!

The Ruby City

What you will need...

Clay
White poster board
Red metallic paper
Colored sponges
Red scouring pad
Small soda straws
Scissors
White glue
Glue stick

*Have you heard of the Emerald City? It is bright green.
We're going to make a cityscape of a ruby-red city!*

Mold a rectangle with the clay. Notice the clay's damp texture.

Press the surface of the clay with the tips of your fingers to change its texture.

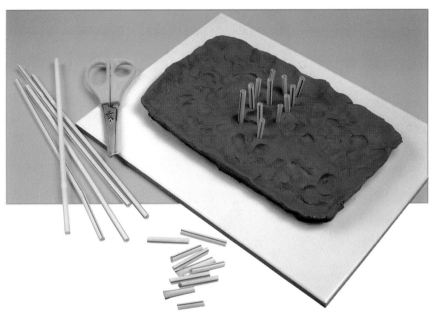

Cut the soda straws into pieces. Push them vertically into the center of the clay before it dries.

The straws are like skyscrapers...

Cut the colored sponges and the red scouring pad into little strips.

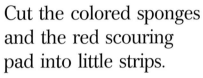

Use the white glue to glue the pieces of colored sponge on one end of the clay rectangle.

...and the sponges will be little houses and shops!

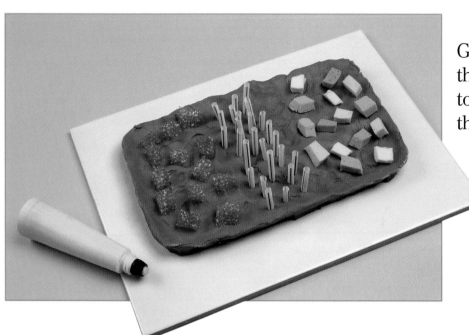

Glue the pieces from the red scouring pad to the other end of the rectangle.

Now we will make a bright red base for the city.

Fold the white poster board in half. Line it with red metallic paper, then glue it onto the clay.

Your Ruby City has tall and pointy skyscrapers, buildings that are smooth and rough, some very bumpy ground, and a shiny red base—what a sight!

TIP

If you don't have a red scouring pad, you can use any color. If you don't have different colored sponges, cut up one of any color and try using markers to make the pieces different colors.

Now That's a Dirty Washcloth!

What you will need...

Brown poster board
White washcloth
Red and green poster paint
Roller
Glue stick
Plastic container

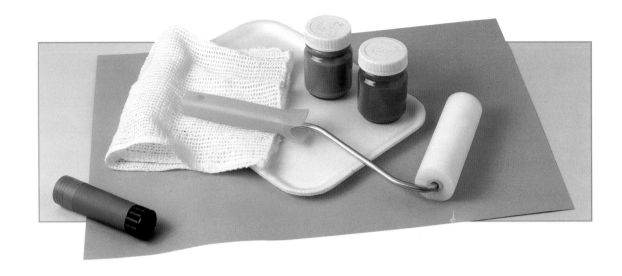

*Washcloths are usually for cleaning . . .
but not this time!*

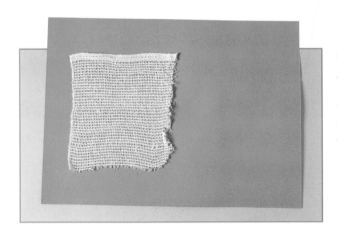

Cut a piece of white washcloth. Place it on one end of the brown poster board.

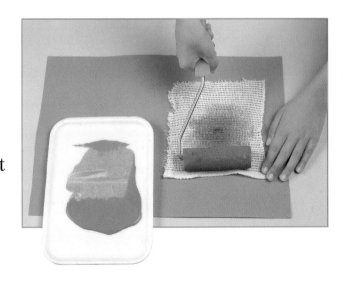

Use the roller to paint the washcloth green.

Rinse the roller, then use it to paint the washcloth red.

When the paint dries, lift the cloth.
The pattern of the weave appears on the paper!

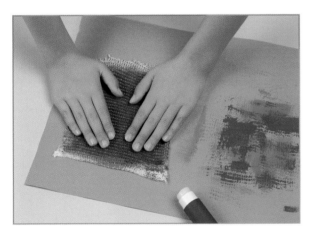

Now glue the painted cloth onto the poster board, next to the patterned stain.

What an unusual piece of art!

YOU CAN TRY
Try making wrapping paper! Use a clean cloth and bright colored paints to make texture stains on regular drawing paper. Once it's dry, you can use your paper to wrap a special gift.

Crazy Train

What you will need...

Green poster board
Three small white plastic bags
Plastic wrap (various colors)
Bubble wrap
Colored plastic twine
Glue stick
Orange poster paint
Paint container
Roller
Scissors

Touch the different materials and compare their textures. How do the different kinds of plastic feel?

Cut two wide strips of bubble wrap. Use the roller to paint them orange. Let them dry.

Crumple up the plastic bags. Shape them into three medium balls.

Roll the colored plastic twine around each of the balls so that they stay round.

Did you notice that these three plastic balls have a smooth, cool texture?

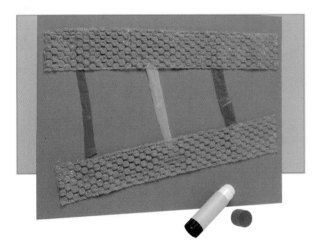

Cut three strips of plastic wrap. Glue them onto the green poster board between the two strips of bubble wrap so that it looks like train tracks.

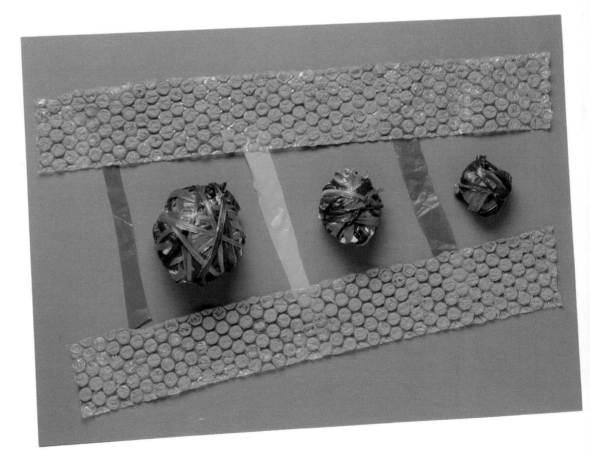

Now place the three balls on the tracks, like the cars of a crazy train!

TIP

If you want, use plastic twine to connect the three balls together. What else can you add to make this more like a real train?

Little House of Textures

What you will need...

Black poster board
Pink and blue paper napkins
Blue and red corrugated cardboard
Strip of foam
Green and orange poster paints
Colored pencils
White pencil
Pencil sharpeners
Thick cord
Glue stick
Scissors
Hole puncher or scissors
Paint container
Small plastic dish or other container
Paintbrush
Tracing paper
Pattern (page 48)

Are you ready to work with more materials to create different textures?

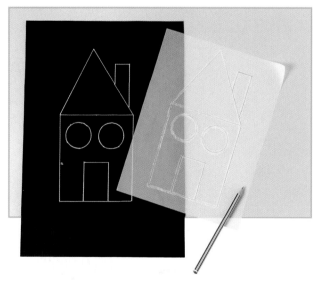

With a white pencil, trace the pattern of the house (page 48) onto the black poster board.

Sharpen the colored pencils. Save all the shavings in the small dish or other container.

Spread a coat of glue for the roof of the house. Glue on the shavings that you saved in the last step.

What an unusual texture this roof will have!

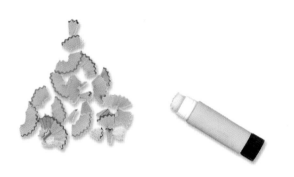

Carefully punch or cut out two round windows for the house.

Cut two small pieces from the paper napkins, each a little bigger than a window. Glue them to the other side of the poster board, behind the windows.

Rub your finger over the windows. How soft they are!

Cut three small pieces from the foam strip. Paint two of them orange and the other one green. When they are dry, glue them onto the door of the house.

What a spongy door!

Also cut four small pieces from the corrugated cardboard, two blue and two red. Glue them onto the chimney.

Finally, cut a piece of the thick cord. Glue it over the chimney for smoke.

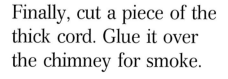

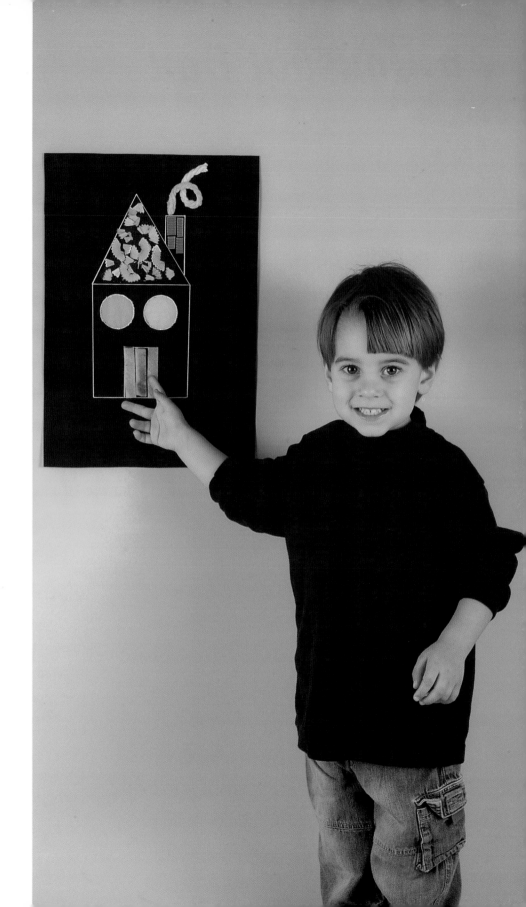

So many textures! You can probably think of other materials to use to make a house with different textures.

TIP
Remember, if you can't find colored corrugated cardboard, just color or paint regular corrugated cardboard any color you like!

An Unusual Doll

What you will need...

Cork board
Round colored stickers
Colored felt
Red cellophane
Green and red shiny paper
Glue stick
Scissors

Notice the texture of the cork.
Compare it with the other materials.

Cut a circle of coated paper for the doll's head. Glue it onto the top part of the cork sheet. Glue small pieces of felt onto it to make eyes, a nose, and a mouth.

Use the colored stickers to make the outline of clothing. Decorate the inside with little colored pieces of felt.

What texture will the other parts of the doll have?

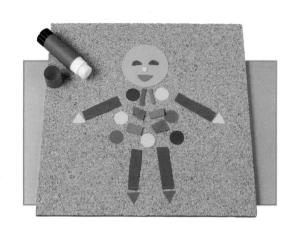

Cut four strips of red coated paper, two for the legs and two for the arms. Glue them on. Make the feet and hands with colored stickers.

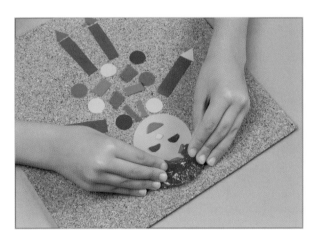

Crumple up a piece of cellophane and glue it on top of the head for hair.

Feel the different parts of the doll. Don't they all have different textures? That is why this is a very unusual doll!

YOU CAN TRY

Try making a friend for your doll! Try using different materials to make another doll, so the first one won't be lonely.

A Special Cake

What you will need . . .
Cardboard box
White, brown, red, yellow, green,
   pink, and orange clay
Toothpicks
Plastic fork
Pencil

*Do you like to bake cakes? This one will be special.
Its "ingredients" are a box and different kinds of clay!*

Coat the top of the cardboard
box with white clay for vanilla
frosting. Use brown clay on the
sides for chocolate.

Mold a ball of red clay and four sticks of different colors: yellow, green, pink, and orange.

Now we will change the texture of the clay...

With a toothpick, trace lines in the brown clay on the sides of the box.

Now use a fork to change the texture of the white clay on the top.

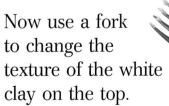

Finally, use the pencil to make holes in the red ball of clay. Make lines on the clay sticks.

Decorate the cake with the sticks and the ball. The texture of this cake might make you want to eat it—but remember, it is only for show!

YOU CAN TRY

Try making other textured "desserts." Try making clay cupcakes with smooth, swirly frosting on top, or clay cookies with bumpy chocolate chips!

"The Sock Collage" by Antoni Tàpies (1923–)

Antoni Tàpies was born in Barcelona, Spain. A museum in Barcelona called the Tàpies Foundation has a great collection of his works.

Tàpies is an artist who experiments with different textures. Aside from paint, you can find cloth, wood, and all kinds of other objects in his paintings.

For example, this work is known as *The Sock Collage* (*El collage del mitjó*). Tàpies used an actual sock to introduce some real-life texture to his painting. Isn't that original?

You can use materials with different textures to create surprising works of art that will amaze everyone. Do you want to give it a try?

Open the Windows!

Pages 12–15

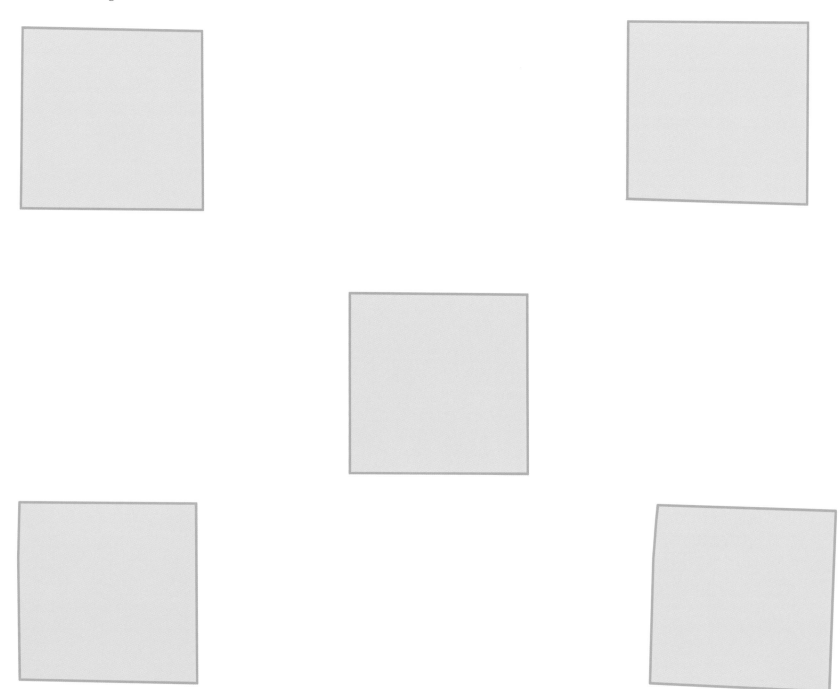

Like a Fish in Water

Pages 22–25

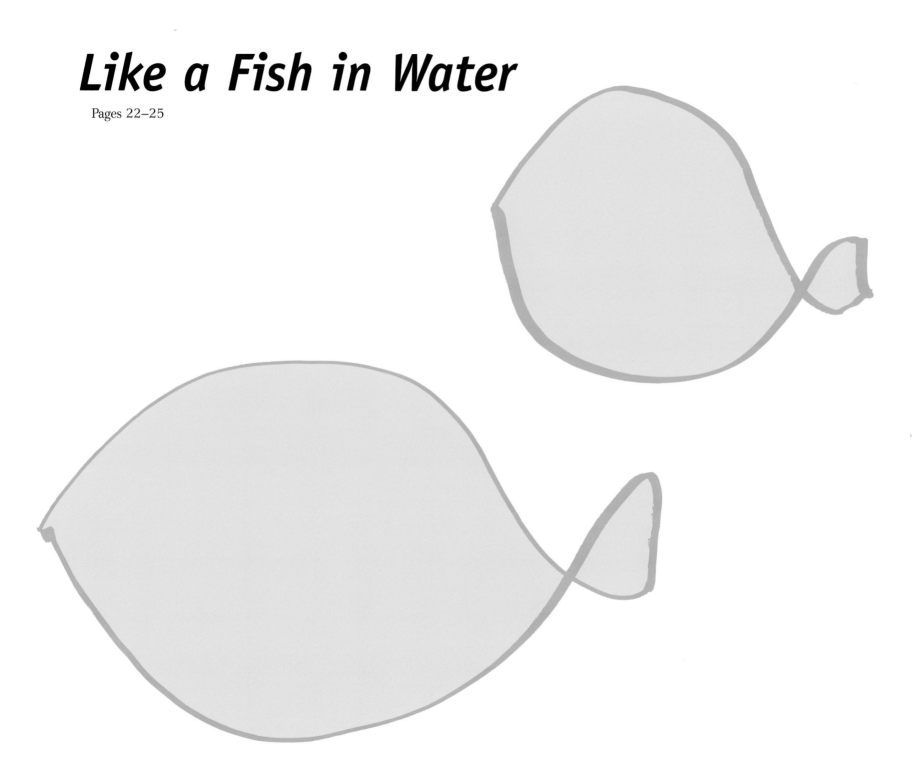

Little House of Textures

Pages 36–39